Late for School

by Claire Llewellyn
illustrated by Moni Perez

 CAMBRIDGE
UNIVERSITY PRESS

 UCL
Institute of Education

The children are going to school.

Leila

Omar

Beno and Hamidi

Zara

They do not want to be late.

Miss Garcia will be cross.

Leila goes to school by bus.
She sits by the window.

'Oh no!' says Leila.

'We are going to be late for school.'

Omar walks to school with Dad and Safiya.

They walk through the park.

Omar stops to look at the fish in the pond.

SPLASH!

'Oh no!' says Dad.

'We are going to be late for school.'

Beno and Hamidi go to school
on the tuk-tuk.

The tuk-tuk stops.

'Oh no!' says Hamidi.

'We are going to be late for school.'

9

Zara goes to school in Dad's car.
The car will not start.

'Oh no!' says Zara.

'We are going to be late for school.'

Miss Garcia goes to school on a bike.

She does not want to be late.

A cat runs into the road.

'Oh no!' says Miss Garcia.

'I am going to be late for school.'

All the children are at school.

Miss Garcia is not at school.

Where is Miss Garcia?

There she is!

Miss Garcia is late for school!

15

Late for School • Claire Llewellyn

Teaching notes written by Sue Bodman and Glen Franklin

Using this book

Developing reading comprehension

This is a book in the International School strand of the Cambridge Reading Adventures which features Omar and his friends. Children may have read others in this series and will know the character traits. In this story, all the characters are worried about being late for school. The twist in the tail is that they all arrive at school before their teacher!

Grammar and sentence structure

- Repetition of phrase patterns, although some variation of structure as events build.
- Oral reading is supported by speech punctuation and exclamations.
- Use of present tense throughout to build tension.

Word meaning and spelling

- Known high frequency words are used in familiar phrases and natural language.
- Opportunity for practise in reading regular decodable words.
- Some unfamiliar vocabulary (*tuk-tuk*) and uses of word tense (*does*) that require attention to letter detail.

Curriculum links

Social Studies – Children can map their journeys to school and chart the different modes of transport used. The topic could also extend to modes of transport around the world, and link with history topics on transport.

Maths – Make graphs and charts of the different ways children in the class travel to school. How long does each journey take?

Learning Outcomes

Children can:

- read more challenging texts using phonic word recognition and knowledge of known high-frequency words
- pay attention to syntax and punctuation to aid reading for meaning
- comment on the events in the story, making links with what is known already about the characters, and children's own experience.

A guided reading lesson

Book Introduction

Give each child a book and read the title to them. If the children have read others in this series (for example, 'Omar's First Day at School', Pink B band; 'Omar Can Help', Red band) talk with them about what they know already of the characters.

Orientation

Give a brief overview of the book, using the present tense structure as it used in the text.

In this story, Omar and his friends are late for school.

Ask the children if they have ever been late for school – what happened that made them late? *Let's find out what happened to make the children late in this story.*

Ask the children to turn to the title page and read the title *'Late for School'* together. Point out the picture and use this to predict what had happened to make Zara late.

Preparation

Pages 2 and 3: Revise the character names, including Miss Garcia who is not depicted on the page.

Pages 4 and 5: Discuss how Leila goes to school. *Why is she going to be late?* Look at page 5: *Leila says 'Oh No!' I think she's really worried, don't you? Let's read this in a worried voice. And what else does she say?* Look for the speech marks: *'We are going to be late for school'. I expect all the other*